DISASTER SCIENCE

WILDFIRES

BY NAOMI CAMERON

Gareth Stevens PUBLISHING

Please visit our website, www.garethstevens.com. For a free color catalog of all our high-quality books, call toll free 1-800-542-2595 or fax 1-877-542-2596.

Cataloging-in-Publication Data
Names: Cameron, Naomi.
Title: Wildfires / Naomi Cameron.
Description: Buffalo, NY : Gareth Stevens Publishing, 2027. | Series: Disaster science | Includes glossary and index.
Identifiers: ISBN 9781482482195 (pbk.) | ISBN 9781482482201 (library bound) | ISBN 9781482482218 (ebook)
Subjects: LCSH: Wildfires--Juvenile literature.
Classification: LCC SD421.23 C364 2027 | DDC 577.2--dc23

Published in 2027
Gareth Stevens Publishing
2544 Clinton Street
Buffalo, NY 14224

Portions of this work were originally authored by Samantha S. Bell and published as *Detecting Wildfires*. All new material in this edition was authored by Naomi Cameron.

Designer: Joshua Olson
Editor: Claire Vanden Branden
Content Consultant: Sen Chiao, PhD, Associate Professor, Meteorology and Climate Science, San José State University

Photo Credits: Cover, pp. 1, 26 Toa55/Shutterstock.com; p. 4 Michala Garrison/NASA; p. 6 Castro and Schnaidt/Shutterstock.com; p. 9 Robert V. Schwemmer/Shutterstock.com; p. 10 Tom Reichner/Shutterstock.com; p. 13 Bizi88/Shutterstock.com; p. 14 B. G. Smith/Shutterstock.com; p. 16 National Archives; p. 19 Kaibab National Forest; p. 21 Michael Woodruff/Shutterstock.com; p. 22 Rob Fly/Shutterstock.com; p. 25 Roger de la Harpe/Shutterstock.com; p. 29 marekuliasz/Shutterstock.com.

Printed in China

CPSIA compliance information: Batch #QS27GS: For further information contact Gareth Stevens at 1-800-542-2595.

TABLE OF CONTENTS

CHAPTER 1

CHILE WILDFIRES

In February 2024, seasonal wildfires are ablaze near the coastal town of Viña del Mar. This city in Chile is home to around 300,000 people. Seasonal wildfires are common in the area. So nearby residents weren't concerned. However, one of the wildfires quickly turned into a disaster.

Smoke from the 2024 Chile wildfire could be seen by satellites in space.

Wildfires can cause widespread destruction. Sometimes cars can burn up.

The wildfire began to spread rapidly. Wind picked up the flames. Fire quickly consumed everything in its path. A wall of black smoke filled the sky.

The fire had followed days of unusually intense heat. The area was in a **drought**.

Then, when strong winds came through, they created a disaster unlike anything Chile had seen before. The fire engulfed nearly 160,000 acres (64,750 ha) of land. Entire neighborhoods were destroyed. Many people went missing, and 131 people died.

2023 CANADIAN WILDFIRES

In 2023, Canada experienced the worst wildfire season ever recorded. Over the course of the year, more than 6,000 wildfires took place. Fires burned 37,065,807 acres (15,000,000 ha) of land. The fires were worsened by temperatures that were higher than usual.

Local firefighters had limited access to water. Some fire hydrants were empty. This prevented firefighters from putting out the fires more quickly. The president of Chile declared a state of emergency. The smoke in the air was dangerous to breathe. Survivors had to **evacuate** their homes.

Scientists believe El Niño played a role in the wildfires. El Niño is a **climate** pattern in the Pacific Ocean that can affect the weather. It brings temperatures that are higher than normal. El Niño tends to happen every two to seven years. In 2024, many countries in South America experienced these higher temperatures. When this heat paired with drought, wind,

Higher-than-average temperatures have led to worse wildfires in many places, including California.

and low humidity, wildfires were just a spark away from taking place.

CHAPTER 2

HOW DO WILDFIRES HAPPEN?

Wildfires are also called wildland fires or forest fires. They occur on every continent except Antarctica. These fires burn in brush, forests, and grasslands. Every year in the United States, there are about 70,000 wildfires.

With wind and dry weather, wildfires can double in size every five minutes.

Wildfires can last for weeks or even months.

These fires can quickly spread and destroy everything in their paths.

Most wildfires are caused by people. Some may leave campfires unattended. They may burn trash or throw used cigarettes on the ground. Occasionally, people start fires on purpose.

Sometimes natural events cause wildfires. Lightning can trigger destructive fires. If a storm knocks over power lines, a spark can start a fire, too.

A wildfire needs oxygen, heat, and fuel. The oxygen comes from the air. The heat comes from fires started by people or nature. The fuel is any material that can burn, such as plants, branches, leaves, and

Lightning is sometimes responsible for starting wildfires.

wooden buildings. Nature keeps the fire going with strong winds, dry weather, and high temperatures.

Wildfires can hurt not only people but also the environment. They pollute the atmosphere with harmful haze and smoke.

Natural wildfires are often healthy for a forest.

Carbon dioxide and other **greenhouse gases** are released into the air. Wildfires burn homes, businesses, and the land where people make their livings. They destroy wildlife habitats and cause soil erosion.

Fire is not always harmful. Sometimes it actually helps the land. The burned plants provide nutrients for the soil. Clearing away trees opens up the **forest floor** to sunlight. This helps other trees grow stronger and healthier.

TYPES OF WILDFIRES

Wildfires are classified into three different categories. Ground fires burn matter in the soil below the forest floor. They are usually started by lightning. Surface fires are the most common. They burn slowly along the forest floor, damaging or killing the trees. Crown fires burn through the tops of trees. They spread quickly in high winds and are often the hardest to contain.

CHAPTER 3

DETECTING WILDFIRES

The US government created the United States Forest Service in 1905. Its policy was to put out wildfires no matter the size or threat. But during the summer of 1910, there were more fires than the Forest Service could handle.

The fires killed 85 people and burned 3 million acres (1.2 million ha) of **timber**.

Two Forest Service workers watch for fires in 1909.

Fire detection became a priority. To help spot wildfires, the government built lookout towers on mountaintops in national forests throughout the United States.

Early fire spotters used the Osborne Firefinder, a device created in 1911 by

THE FIRST WOMAN LOOKOUT

In 1913, Hallie M. Daggett started working at a lookout station on Klamath Peak in the Klamath National Forest. This forest is on the border of California and Oregon. Every summer for 15 years, she sat alone in the tower, watching for fires. Her sister would bring supplies and mail once a week. Hallie did not mind the storms or the wild animals. She enjoyed the job and was happy to join the fight against wildfires.

The Osborne Firefinder looks like a round glass table. A map on the surface shows the surrounding land.

William Bushnell Osborne Jr. By sighting distant smoke in the Firefinder, spotters could determine the location of a forest fire. Firefinders are still used in some places today.

Rural telephones also helped officials detect wildfires. The Forest Service's first telephone line was constructed in 1906 in Wyoming. Telephones provided better communication for spotters and forest rangers.

Just after World War I (1914–1918), the Forest Service joined with the Army Air Service to provide airplanes and pilots to spot wildfires from the air. The program worked well for more than 10 years. By the 1930s, a large system of lookout towers and telephones was ready to take its place.

Spotting fires from lookout towers usually works well. But a spotter's view can be limited by clouds or fog. And watching

Lookouts often lived in their towers for weeks at a time.

for fires for days at a time can be boring and tiring. Today, only a few hundred lookout stations are still used in the United States.

CHAPTER 4

TODAY'S WARNING SYSTEMS

Improvements in technology have led to advanced systems for detecting wildfires. Some systems use video cameras. The cameras are usually mounted on a tower close to a potential fire source. The cameras can detect smoke and fire within the surrounding 116 square miles (300 sq km).

Some lookout towers now have cameras mounted on them.

Some cameras have sensors that estimate the location, size, speed, and direction of a fire.

Wildfires are still detected from above, too. Spotters may fly airplanes to help find and fight fires. The higher the planes go, the larger the area the spotters can search. **Satellite** systems cover even wider areas.

In 2015, forestry officials began using **drones** to detect wildfires. The first one was used during the Paradise Fire in Washington's Olympic National Park. The drone gathered information when conditions were too smoky to use piloted airplanes. The drone used **infrared**

Spotter planes can help firefighters plan the best ways to fight wildfires.

technology to find how widely the fire had spread and where the heat was most intense.

Firefighter safety is the main reason drones are used. But there are other reasons, too. Drones can fly at any time.

Some drones can spray chemicals onto a wildfire to help slow it down.

They can even fly at night. They can get much closer to fires than people can. Plus, drones are much cheaper to use than helicopters and pilots.

Drones can collect data on the speed and spread of a fire. When officials have this information, they can make better decisions. So early detection is important. Officials need to find out whether people will be in danger. They must determine if a fire is small enough to manage or if they should try to put it out. They know that the larger a wildfire grows before it is detected, the harder it is to fight.

FACT FILE

WILDFIRE SAFETY

If you live somewhere that is at risk for wildfires, there are several steps you can take to stay safe. Prepare an emergency kit with a flashlight, batteries, money, and first aid supplies.

Prepare your home in case a wildfire comes near. Clean the roof and gutters regularly. Make sure to clear away objects that could burn, such as piles of wood or brush.

If you see a wildfire and have not received evacuation orders yet, call 911. Don't assume someone else has already called to report the fire. Then listen to the radio and watch the TV for news and emergency instructions.

If you are ordered to evacuate, make sure to tell someone where you and your family are going.

Fire danger rating signs warn people how likely wildfires are to start and spread.

Return home only after the authorities declare your area safe.

If you get burned by a fire, call 911 or find medical help quickly. Cool the burn with clean running water, and cover it to prevent infections.

TEST YOUR KNOWLEDGE

Take this quiz to test your knowledge.

1. Write a paragraph outlining the major ways in which people detect wildfires.

2. Would you want to work in a wildfire lookout tower? Why or why not?

3. Which wildfire-detecting devices are used in lookout towers?

    A. Osborne Firefinders
    B. drones
    C. satellites

4. Why are drones with infrared technology useful for detecting fires?

    A. People aboard can spot a fire.
    B. The drones can detect heat.
    C. The drones can predict where a fire might start.

Answers can be found on page 32.

GLOSSARY

climate
The average weather conditions of a particular place or region.

drones
Remote-controlled aircraft without pilots.

drought
A period of time with little or no rain.

evacuate
To leave a place of danger.

forest floor
The upper layer of soil and decaying matter in a forest.

greenhouse gases
Gases that trap heat in Earth's atmosphere, causing climate change.

infrared
Light that is invisible to human eyes but can be seen by certain cameras.

satellite
A spacecraft that orbits Earth, often to collect information.

timber
Trees grown for their wood.

FOR MORE INFORMATION

BOOKS

Jaycox, Jaclyn. *Wildfires*. North Mankato, MN: Pebble, 2022.

Murray, Julie. *Wildfires*. Minneapolis, MN: Abdo Publishing, 2025.

WEBSITES

Britannica Kids: Wildland Fire
kids.britannica.com/kids/article/wildland-fire/625005
Learn more about how wildfires can start.

Western Fire Chiefs Association: 10 Wildfire Facts for Kids
wfca.com/wildfire-articles/wildfire-facts-for-kid/
Learn more interesting facts about wildfires.

Publisher's note to educators and parents: Our editors have carefully reviewed these websites to ensure that they are suitable for students. Many websites change frequently, however, and we cannot guarantee that a site's future contents will continue to meet our high standards of quality and educational value. Be advised that students should be closely supervised whenever they access the internet.

INDEX

Answer Key: 1. Answers will vary; 2. Answers will vary; 3. A; 4. B